AMELIA ISLAND
MUSEUM
OF **HISTORY**

UNLOCK THE PAST

Meet me on™

AMELIA ISLAND

Copyright © 2013 by
Southwestern Publishing Group, Inc.

Published by

An imprint of

P.O. Box 305142
Nashville, Tennessee 37230
1-800-358-0560
www.historichospitalitybooks.com

Publisher and President: Dave Kempf
Editorial Director: Mary Cummings
Art Director and Book Design:
Starletta Polster

Library of Congress Control Number:
2013946402
ISBN: 978-0-87197-595-9

Amelia Island editor: Dickie Anderson
Recipe editors: Lisa Waas and Judy Pillans
Photography: © Stephan Leimberg

Additional photography: Omni Amelia
Island Plantation, Ritz–Carlton, Amelia
Island, the Golf Club of Amelia.

Historic home photographs from *Great
Homes of Fernandina—Architectural
Treasures from Amelia Island's Golden
Age,* Jan Johannes

Illustration and Photography: Sea Oats ©
Thinkstock

AMELIA ISLAND
MUSEUM
OF HISTORY
UNLOCK THE PAST

Meet me on™
AMELIA ISLAND

TIMELESS IMAGES AND FLAVORFUL RECIPES
FROM FLORIDA'S REMARKABLE AMELIA ISLAND

INTRODUCTION

Dear Reader,

In creating our *Historic Hospitality*™ series of books, it is my sincere desire, as publisher, to present beautifully crafted books that relate the cherished history of each geographic area, highlight beautiful historic and contemporary photography, and offer delicious recipes unique to the area. These make the perfect memoir of your visit or a very special gift for a friend. We are proud to include historic Amelia Island as one of our featured Historic Hospitality sites.

It is our pleasure to share the story of Amelia Island with you.

Sincerely,

David J. Kempf

Dave Kempf
Southwestern Publishing Group, Inc.

OMNI AMELIA ISLAND PLANTATION

Meet Me On Amelia Island

Amelia Island, the northernmost of Florida's barrier islands, offers a rare combination of natural beauty and luxurious accommodations. Home to the Omni Amelia Island Plantation and the Ritz–Carlton, Amelia Island, the island is a much sought-after destination. It has it all—championship golf courses, clay tennis courts, beautiful parks, a 13-mile beach, and miles of bicycle-friendly paths.

The island's best kept secret may be its sleepy little town of Fernandina Beach. Frozen in time, the town is nestled in a 50-square block historic district located on the north end. Whether you are a dedicated shopper or a history buff, you will find something to delight you. A rare find in this day and age of shopping malls, the town's main street is lined with unique shops and restaurants, all locally owned. You can buy homemade fudge, ice cream, original art, books, gifts of all kinds, antiques, jewelry, seashore treasures, and T-shirts. Of course, there is a Christmas shop. Shopkeepers offer a friendly greeting and are eager ambassadors for their community. The town takes on a magical persona when the sun goes down and twinkling white lights illuminate the trees that line Centre Street.

Just a few blocks off Centre Street, you can walk through a living museum of elegant Victorian "painted ladies," the Historic District's beautifully preserved homes with their elaborate gingerbread trim and unusual colors. The harbor overlooks the Amelia River and Intracoastal Waterway. Picturesque shrimp boats line the river's edge.

Enjoy fine dining or, perhaps, one of the downtown's more casual restaurants. Amelia Island has it all. No matter the length of stay, you will find new and interesting places to eat—from seafood to unique gourmet specialties. Many local restaurants offer

entertainment. The island has two active community theaters and a wide variety of musical offerings.

Amelia Island is truly one of the best-kept secrets for those seeking the gentle beauty of a coastal island, the very best in accommodations, and the charm of a history well-preserved and celebrated. Try Amelia Island—you'll keep coming back.

11

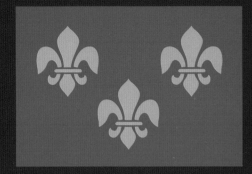

FRENCH FLAG

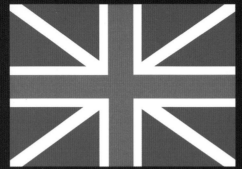

BRITISH FLAG

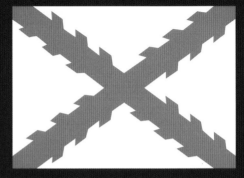

SPANISH BURGUNDY CROSS FLAG

SALUS POPULI LEX SUPREMA

PATRIOT FLAG

GREGOR MACGREGOR'S
GREEN CROSS FLAG

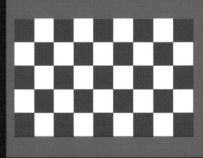

LUIS AURY'S MEXICAN
REBEL FLAG

Eight Flags Over One Island

Amelia Island was the home of the indigenous Timucuan Indians for thousands of years. They were a handsome and healthy people. Then came the Europeans, and the diseases they brought wiped out the ancient tribe in frighteningly short time. Next came four hundred years of history with eight flags. Amelia Island is the only place in the United States that can make such a boast. With its prized geographic location and deep natural harbor, Amelia Island has been fought over and swapped for hundreds of years. It is said that the French visited, the Spanish developed, the English named, and the Americans tamed.

The French were the first Europeans who hoped to establish a colony in north Florida in 1562. Their small colony lasted a short time and ended tragically. The Spanish massacred most of the French living in the first settlement. Spain continued to dominate much of Florida and Amelia Island's early history. In the First Treaty of Paris, 1814, England swapped Cuba for Florida and for a brief time the British flag flew over the island. With the Second Treaty of Paris, the swap reversed, and the island and Florida returned to the Spanish.

With each flag came a new name. The French called the island Isle de Mai. Later Spain dubbed it Santa Maria. Although it was still a Spanish possession, James Oglethorpe, while visiting, named the island Amelia after the youngest daughter of King George II. The name remains.

As Spain's dominance ebbed, a series of flags ran up and down island flag poles. These included the Patriot Flag, Gregor MacGregor's Green Cross Flag, and, for a brief time, pirate Luis Aury's Mexican Rebel Flag. Spain ceded Florida to the United States in 1821, and, except for a brief time during the Civil War, the red white and blue has proudly flown.

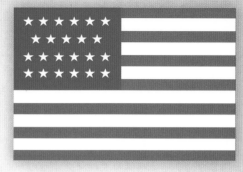

UNITED STATES FLAG, 1821

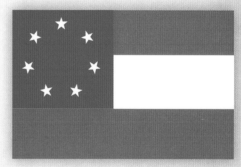

CONFEDERACY 1ST NATIONAL FLAG

AMELIA ISLAND'S "MAIN STREET"

Fernandina Beach's Centre Street is a charming throwback to a quieter, gentler time in Amelia Island's history. Anchored by a picturesque harbor, Centre Street is eight blocks long and lined with vintage brick buildings dating back to the late 1800s. Welcoming businesses include bookstores, coffee shops, antique shops, craft and clothing stores, cozy dining spots, and watering holes. Just off Centre Street are more shops and the historic Florida House Inn, now a bed and breakfast.

Benches under umbrellas of shade trees invite visitors to sit and enjoy the ambience of small town America. The stately courthouse, elegant post office, the historic Lesesne house, and old train depot add to the small town's charm. Inviting pocket parks are tucked between historic buildings.

The Palace Saloon is a favorite tourist destination. Promoted as the oldest continually operating saloon in Florida, the wonderful old bar reminds visitors of what it might be like to visit a gentleman's bar in the late 1800s. The life-size pirate standing guard is a favorite photo op for visitors.

A lively farmers market is offered each Saturday morning just off Centre on North 7th Street. The market is a popular meeting place for islanders and visitors to enjoy a chance to slow down, meet neighbors, and purchase the freshest of produce, baked goods, and plants.

COKE SIGN — CENTRE STREET

AMELIA COMMUNITY THEATRE
3RD & CEDAR ST.

FLORIDA HOUSE INN
FOOD · LODGING · SPIRITS

Slightly Off Centre
one block south

bright mornings
a bakery cafe

Amelia San Jon
Fine Art Gallery

Amelia Island
Museum of History   3 BLOCKS

THE HAPPY TOMATO
Courtyard Cafe & BBQ

Kelley's Courtyard Café

29 South
Restaurant

FLORIDA'S OLDEST BAR

PALACE SALOON PIRATE

SIGNS FOR CENTRE AND
OFF-CENTRE STREET

Nature's Playground

Amelia Island offers an amazing variety of ways to explore and enjoy its beaches, marshes, and parks. Opportunities abound to explore by boat, car, bicycle, or on foot.

Located at the far north end of Amelia Island, Fort Clinch State Park offers a myriad of activities as well its historic fort. Sunbathing, swimming, and beachcombing are popular activities. Anglers can fish from the pier or take advantage of excellent surf fishing. Hikers and bicyclists can enjoy a six-mile trail through the park. Self-guided nature trails provide opportunities to learn about and observe native plants and wildlife. A full-facility campground and a youth camping area provide overnight accommodations.

The Talbot islands off the south end of Amelia Island are among the few remaining undeveloped barrier islands in Northeast Florida. The islands offer miles of beautiful, white sandy beaches, lush maritime forests, desert-like dunes, and undisturbed salt marshes. Both kayaking and horseback riding on the beach are available.

On Amelia Island, Egan's Creek Greenway offers 300 acres of protected land along a scenic tidal creek.The natural setting, with its grass-covered trails, is ideal for hiking, biking, dog walking, and wildlife and nature observation and photography.

Amelia Island is bicycle friendly. The Talbot Island trail segments and the Amelia Island Trail provide 14.8 miles of safe bicycle riding. This coastal trail through Amelia Island and the Talbot Islands is part of the East Coast Greenway, which is a planned coastal bike trail from Maine to the Florida Keys.

For water adventure, there are lots of options which include surfing, kayaking, paddle boarding, sailing, and fishing. Amelia River Cruises and Charters offers a variety

ANHINGA

16

of popular, narrated sightseeing cruises.

Amelia Island is ideally located for a variety of fishing adventures. You can fish from a pier, bridge, or boat or charter one of the many boats that offer fishing with backwater or open sea options.

The more adventurous can see the island from the air by choosing an airplane tour, or a hang-gliding or a parachuting adventure.

RIGHT: TURTLES
BOTTOM: ARMADILLO

OMNI AMELIA ISLAND PLANTATION
A GRAND REIMAGINING

In 1971, forward-thinking developer, Charles Fraser, planned a community that would balance the preservation of Amelia Island's natural beauty with the creation of a luxurious gated residential community and resort destination. Purchasing a large tract of land from Union Carbide, Fraser was able to maximize the development of the island's then unspoiled natural beauty which includes 3.5 miles of pristine beach. The result, the Amelia Island Plantation, was a master plan designed to protect tidal marshes and conserve oceanfront dunes, grass land, and savannahs.

Omni Hotels & Resorts, with its purchase of the Amelia Island Plantation, continues the commitment to preserve and appreciate the island's natural environment. On property naturalists are available at the resort's Nature Center. There is a shop with exhibits and a chance to meet some island creatures. Tours can be scheduled.

Omni Amelia Island Plantation has been ranked as one of the top 121 golf resorts in the world by Conde Nast Traveler. Its three golf courses offer views of tidal marshes, the Intracoastal Waterway, and the Atlantic Ocean. In keeping with Omni Amelia Island Plantation's commitment to the environment, the courses are Audubon International Certified Sanctuaries.

The Omni Amelia Island Plantation Resort tennis program is operated by Cliff Drysdale Tennis. Since 1974, guests and professionals have been enjoying this prestigious tennis facility set beneath a canopy of majestic live oaks and offering 23 premium fast-dry clay courts. Many legends of tennis have played at Omni

Amelia Island Plantation including Andre Agassi, Martina Navratilova, Chris Evert, Martina Hingis, Maria Sharapova, and the Williams sisters.

The renovation that opened in 2013 included the dramatic "Re-Imagination" of the main hotel. Guests immediately interact with water from an elevated porte cochere and lobby with floor-to-ceiling windows overlooking fire and water features, and, of course, the Atlantic Ocean. The resort offers nine restaurants and lounges with Southern-style flare, farm-to-table dining, and fresh seafood.

Whether one is bringing a conference group, planning a family vacation or romantic get-away, Omni Amelia Island Plantation has something for everyone.

Amelia Island's Victorian Treasures

"Exploring Amelia Island's Historic District is to experience another time and place. Like sleeping beauties, Amelia Island's painted Victorian ladies have been frozen in time. The late 1800s were truly a Golden Age for Florida's most northern barrier island." —*Great Homes of Fernandina, Architectural Treasures from Amelia Island's Golden Age*

THE BAILEY HOUSE

The Bailey House is considered one of the most outstanding examples of Victorian period architecture in Florida and is a favorite subject for both photographers and painters. It is one of many "bride houses" on the island. Effingham Bailey built the beautiful house on the corner of Ash and 7th Streets for his bride, Kate MacDonnell. Its design features a wide variety of architectural elements. It is a feast for the eyes with its contrasting colors that highlight gables, turrets and windows of all sizes and shapes and unique fish scale shingles.

THE TABBY HOUSE

This unusual house is constructed of tabby and is the only house of its kind remaining on the island. The method of construction is simple: a mixture of Portland cement and oyster shells is poured into molds to create the walls of a house. The horizontal lines that indicate the individual sections of wall are clearly visible. It took three years to build the house. The detailed trim on the galleries is typical of the intricate detail that Robert Sands Schuyler, renowned island architect, included in his architectural designs. Similar detailing can be seen in the Williams House, the Old School House, and St. Peter's Episcopal Church.

THE HOYT HOUSE

Set back and sheltered by enormous live oaks the Hoyt House has been a family home, a lawyer's office and currently operates as a bed and breakfast inn. The Hoyt House is said to be modeled after one of the cottages built on Jekyll Island. It has been cited in the National Register of Historic Places as "noteworthy for its octagonal two-story bay, cross gable, balcony, hip-roof, hip-dormers and bracketed eaves." Its interior is crafted out of the finest heart of pine and oak. Each of its seven coal burning fireplaces has a beautiful carved mantel.

FAIRBANKS HOUSE

The Fairbanks House, in all her elegant Italianate beauty, ages gracefully on Fernandina Beach's South 7th Street. Her colors are very close to the originals that were fashionable so long ago. Her mustard yellow is accented by deep green and brick red, the same colors first chosen by George Fairbanks when he built the house in 1885 for his second wife. The bones are classic: elegant balustrade porches, dormers, bay windows, massive chimneys, an oriel window and the tower reaching into the sky. It currently operates as a bed and breakfast inn.

THE WILLIAMS HOUSE

This antebellum home, one of several in the Historic District, is a two and a half story frame vernacular with second-story veranda and elaborate turned detail. The interior stairway is decorated with five stained glass windows. The original pre-Civil War house was simple in design. At a later time, additional exterior design work was done by architect Robert Sands Schuyler. The porch detail is so unusual and house-defining, Schuyler agreed in writing not to duplicate the striking design. It currently operates as a bed and breakfast inn.

WILLIAM BELL HOUSE
BEECH STREET GRILL

For many years the house built in 1889 operated as the popular Beech Street Grill. Described as East Lake and Chinese Chippendale, the house, like so many Victorian houses in the Historic District, is a mix of many different styles and periods depending on the whims and ideas of the builder. The house was built by William Bell, one of the Bell brothers and a harbor pilot as a "bride" house for his wife.

Fort Clinch—The Fort that Never Saw a Battle

FRANK OFELDT—
FORT CLINCH STATE PARK
RE-ENACTOR

Amelia Island's Fort Clinch State Park is truly an island treasure. A large portion of the northern end of the island is parkland and offers a variety of experiences including a tour of its historic fort. The park is located on a peninsula surrounded by Egan's Creek, the Amelia River, and the Atlantic Ocean.

For history buffs, the fort is a well-preserved 19th century brick fortress. Begun in 1847, it remained a work in progress as the soldiers stationed there continued to add to the intricate brickwork throughout the fort. There were never any battles or fatalities. During the Civil War when Federal troops arrived on Amelia Island, the Confederate troops simply caught the first train out of town. On the first weekend of each month, costumed interpreters perform living history re-enactments demonstrating what it might have been like for the soldiers and their families occupying the fort.

After a history lesson, an amazing array of recreational options await those who explore the beautiful park with its plethora of tidal creeks, expansive beaches, and grand old oak trees. The half mile pier offers a dramatic view or, perhaps, the perfect fishing spot. There is camping, exploring by foot or bicycle, or taking a segway tour.

Aerial view of Fort Clinch

THE LIGHTHOUSE—ISLAND ICON

What is an island without a lighthouse? Like any good island, Amelia Island has an official, working often photographed, lighthouse. Located on the north end of the island, visitors can catch a glimpse of it driving west on Atlantic Avenue. It sits high atop the highest point on the island overlooking Egan's Creek. It has the standard lighthouse profile—but is missing the black stripe often associated with a lighthouse.

The lighthouse, built in 1838, boasts a long and intriguing history. In the years when Florida was still under Spanish rule, the United States established a lighthouse at what was then the most southernmost site on the coast of the United States—Cumberland Island. In 1821, the Spanish ceded Florida to the United States, and it was decided Amelia Island would be a better place for the beacon. The lighthouse was moved!

It is Florida's oldest lighthouse, and the only one from the Territorial Period, that has survived without major rebuilding. When the lantern first sent its beam out to sea, Florida was not yet a state. Strategically placed near the St. Mary's River, a major waterway, the light has guided wooden hulled sailing ships and, later, freighters, shrimp boats, and fishing boats.

The City of Fernandina Beach received possession of the lighthouse from the U.S. Coast Guard in 2001.The Coast Guard, with the help of Auxiliary volunteers, is responsible for the function of the beacon. Tours are offered twice monthly on Wednesdays.

THE RITZ–CARLTON, AMELIA ISLAND
A COASTAL TREASURE

Perched above a pristine, dune-lined beach, the Ritz–Carlton, Amelia Island offers a seaside setting that is an ideal backdrop for creating cherished memories and traditions. In addition to more than a mile of beach, the resort offers an 18-hole championship golf course, a spa and full-service beauty salon, a 24-hour fitness center, special programs for kids, and on-site tennis facilities.

A signature of The Ritz–Carlton, Amelia Island is the theme of salt. The AAA Five Diamond restaurant, Salt, features simple ingredients from the earth and the sea, properly seasoned and artfully prepared. When the hotel's oceanfront restaurant was being remodeled, a team determined that salt embodied a sense of place; with the Atlantic on one side and tidal marshes and rivers on the other, the restaurant was surrounded by "salt." The award-winning restaurant is renowned for its masterful pairing of salts from around the world with each course.

Salt is incorporated in many of the services offered by the hotel's spa, utilizing Himalayan salts, known for their purest, totally natural, unrefined and cleaning attributes treatments that cleanse, detoxify, and improve the skin's elasticity. The Salt Shop, located just off the lobby, offers over forty varieties of gourmet natural and infused salts from all over the world.

Whether it's a walk on the island's 13 mile beach or enjoying one of the hotel's pools, relaxation is assured. Minutes from the hotel is Amelia Island's Historic District with its unique shops, beautiful harbor, and a virtual living museum of beautiful

Victorian homes. The hotel concierge can arrange for horseback riding on the beach, backwater or deep sea fishing excursions, or a reservation at one of the island's unique restaurants.

The Ritz–Carlton, Amelia Island offers its world class service on one of Florida's most beautiful coastal islands

Amelia Island Concours d'Elegance

Car lovers and collectors gather on the second weekend in March each year for the Amelia Island Concours d'Elegance, an automotive charitable event held at the Golf Club of Amelia adjacent to the Ritz–Carlton, Amelia Island. A New York Times article about celebrity car ownership listed the event as one of the top events in the country and of the same caliber as the famed Pebble Beach car event in California.

A Concours d'Elegance (French, literally "a competition of elegance") is, according to New York Times writer Keith Martin, like a "beauty pageant for rare and elegant cars." Each entry is examined and rated for authenticity, function, history, style, and quality of restoration by a team of judges that includes specialists for each car type.

Bill Warner, a photographer and writer for Road & Track magazine since 1971 and an avid car collector, founded the Amelia Island Concours d'Elegance in 1996 at the urging of other northeast Florida auto enthusiasts who envisioned a classic car show in Florida like the Pebble Beach Concours d'Elegance.

Each year's Amelia Island Concours honors an outstanding person from motor sports, a featured Marque (manufacturer) or theme, plus judging and awards for each class of the Field of Dreams, the showcase exhibition. Other events may vary each year but have included a golf tournament, automobile auctions, art and fashion shows, silent auctions of memorabilia, charity raffles, and autograph sessions.

Many of the competing cars are valued in the hundreds of thousands of dollars, with some worth millions. For this reason, along with its remarkable setting and amenities, the Amelia Island Concours is considered one of the premier car shows in the world.

An Island That Loves Festivals

Amelia Island has proved a perfect place to stage a festival. Each year the island celebrates the Amelia Island Chamber Music Festival, the Amelia Island Jazz Festival, the Amelia Island Blues Festival, the Amelia Island Film Festival, and the Amelia Island Book Festival. In addition, Wild Amelia is an annual festival that celebrates the natural beauty of the area. The island's convenient location and reputation for supporting the arts has created the perfect environment for a variety of groups celebrating their particular genre of music or interest.

When it comes to celebrating, nothing is bigger, better, or badder than the Annual Isle of Eight Flags Shrimp Festival. It is Amelia Island's own Mardi Gras. The island explodes with activity as crowds gather for the annual festival celebrated on the first weekend of May each year. Why shrimp? Amelia Island is the recognized birthplace of the modern shrimping industry in the United States

Traditionally, a small town parade kicks off the festival. Friday night, Centre Street and its side streets are blocked off as more than 300 juried artists and crafts people move in to prepare for the crowds that arrive Saturday and Sunday. Three stages, as well as some of the local bars and eateries, offer foot stomping music. Kids flock to activities just for them. On Sunday, the street sales continue, and there is a traditional blessing of the shrimp fleet and a prize for the best decorated shrimp boat. Colorful pirates wander the streets giving out beads and candy to the children.

Whether its the quiet sophistication of a symphony orchestra, the intimacy of chamber music, foot-tapping jazz, moody blues, best-selling authors, entertaining films or the island's annual celebration of shrimp—Amelia Island something for everyone.

ARTWORK AT THE ISLE OF EIGHT FLAGS ANNUAL SHRIMP FESTIVAL 2013

JACKSONVILLE SYMPHONY ORCHESTRA

ISLE OF EIGHT FLAGS ANNUAL SHRIMP FESTIVAL 2013

Weekend Fun at American Beach

AMERICAN BEACH
A SPECIAL PIECE OF BEACH

American Beach is part of Amelia Island's unique and special history. It was founded in 1935 by Florida's first black millionaire, Abraham Lincoln Lewis, and his Afro-American Life Insurance Company. Before desegregation, it offered a beach where black families could vacation and own homes. Throughout the 30s, 40s and 50s, American Beach was the scene of family fun. There were hotels, restaurants, and night clubs that hosted celebrities including Zora Neale Hurston, Cab Calloway, Billy Eckstein, Ray Charles and James Brown.

In 1964 Hurricane Dora did great damage to Amelia Island, and many homes and buildings were lost on American Beach. In the same year, the Civil Rights Act was passed and the beaches of Florida were desegregated. Things began to change for the beachside community.

MaVynee Betsch, the eccentric great-granddaughter of A. L. Lewis, known locally as the "Beach Lady," dedicated herself to preserving American Beach and fighting pressure from neighboring resort properties. The tallest sand dune in Florida is a protected landmark due largely to the efforts of Betsch. The 60-foot dune system that she dubbed "NaNa" and the adjoining property to the shoreline is now a national park and included in the Timucuan Ecological and Historic Preserve.

Many houses in American Beach are still in the families of the original owners. Residents remain fiercely proud of their history and community. Since January 2002, American Beach has been listed as a historic site by the National Register of Historic Places.

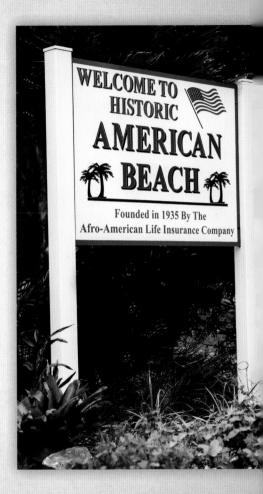

American Beach Flag Cake

2   *pints fresh strawberries*
1½ *cups boiling water*
1   *8-serving package strawberry or cherry flavored gelatin*
1   *cup cold water*
1   *12-ounce pound cake, cut into 10 slices*
1½ *cups fresh blueberries, divided*
1   *8-ounce tub whipped topping*

Slice 1 cup of strawberries; halve the remaining strawberries.

Stir the boiling water into gelatin in a bowl until completely disolved. Mix cold water and enough ice to make 2 cups. Stir into the gelatin until the ice is melted. Refrigerate for 5 minutes or until slightly thickened.

Line an 8 x 12-inch dish with cake slices. Stir the sliced strawberries and 1 cup blueberries into the gelatin. Spoon evenly over the cake. Refrigerate for 4 hours or until firm. Spread the whipped topping over gelatin. Arrange strawberry halves and remaining blueberries on top to create a flag.

Serves 16

Alexander Hickson from Marsha Phelts, *The American Beach Cookbook*

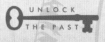

UNLOCK
THE PAST

Cioppino

3/4 cup butter
2 onions, chopped
2 cloves of garlic, minced
1 bunch fresh parsley, chopped
2 14.5 ounce cans stewed tomatoes
2 14.5 ounce cans chicken broth
2 bay leaves
1 tablespoon dried basil
1/2 teaspoon dried thyme

1/2 teaspoon dried oregano
1 cup water
1 1/2 cups white wine
1 1/2 pounds shrimp, peeled and deveined
18 scallops
18 small clams
18 mussels, cleaned and debearded
1 1/2 cups crab meat
1 1/2 pounds cod fillets (optional)

Melt butter over medium-low heat in a large stockpot. Add onions, garlic, and parsley. Cook slowly, until onions are soft, stirring occasionally. Add tomatoes to the pot, breaking them into chunks as you add them. Add chicken broth, bay leaves, basil, thyme, oregano, water and wine. Cover and simmer for 30 minutes. (This stock can be prepared early in the day and reheated.) Stir in shrimp, scallops, clams, mussels, and crab meat. Stir in fish, if desired. Bring to a boil. Lower heat, cover, and simmer for 5 to 7 minutes or until clams open. Ladle into bowls and enjoy with warm, crusty bread.

Yield: 8 to 10 servings

The Golf Club of Amelia Island

AMELIA'S CAMELLIAS

When spring comes to Amelia and the azaleas, redbud, and dogwood bloom, Gus Gerbing is probably smiling. Gustav George Gerbing was born in 1900 and grew up on Amelia Island. Ever the entrepreneur, he opened a seafood restaurant at the young age of 19 and became a successful oysterman. His success as a businessman allowed him to pursue his first love, horticulture. A self-taught plantsman, he was always learning from what he saw as he traveled through the Southeast selling oysters and plants. He was so impressed with the beauty of Magnolia Gardens in Charleston, South Carolina, that he determined that he would create a similar tourist draw on Amelia Island. Gerbing passionately pursued his lifelong passion of the propagation of hundreds of camellias and azaleas. In 1947 there was a spectacular opening of Gerbing Gardens. Hundreds visited the gardens and enjoyed the Festival of Flowers complete with beauty queens. His plantings were spread over fifteen acres where Amelia City is today. When his fortunes reversed, the land was sold and divided, and through the years became overgrown.

Fortunately, seven acres of Gerbing's original camellia and azalea grove survive as one parcel. Private owners purchased a large piece of the original property and have saved many of the plants that had survived. With the active support of the homeowners, more than 1000 camellia specimens have been photographed and tagged. In 2011 the International Camellia Society, the American Camellia Society, and the Great Gardens Preservation Alliance gathered on the island and identified some of the original plantings of Gus Gerbing. Because of the historical importance of Gerbing Gardens as a public garden, and its cultural significance in the history of Florida, it is listed in the Archives of American Gardens at the Smithsonian Institution.

Gerbings GARDENS

FERNANDINA BEACH, FLA.

CALENDULAS SURROUND POOL

COPYRIGHT MCMXLVII BY CURT TEICH

"NORTH FLORIDA'S MAJOR TOURIST ATTRA

Sunken Gardens, Gerbings Gardens, Fernandina Beach, Fla.

Seared Tuna with Tartar Dressing and Pineapple Salsa

6 to 8 ounce tuna fillets,
one per person

Salt and pepper to taste
1 teaspoon oil

Season tuna with salt and pepper mixture. Heat 1 teaspoon oil in a hot pan and sear each side of tuna for about two minutes. Slice each fillet into about seven slices. Brush with tartar dressing. Spoon pineapple salsa over tuna. Serve with rice.

PINEAPPLE SALSA
2 1/2 cups pineapple, ¼ inch dice
1/3 cup red onion, medium dice
2 tablespoons fresh lime juice
1/4 teaspoon kosher salt
3 tablespoons jalapeño, seeded and minced
2 tablespoons cilantro, rough chopped

TARTAR DRESSING
1/3 cup ginger oil
1/4 cup wasabi paste
1/4 cup green onions, white part only, minced fine
2 tablespoons jalapeno, seeds removed and minced fine
1/4 cup fresh cilantro, minced fine
1/2 cup fresh lime juice
1/2 cup vegetable oil
1 teaspoon Sriracha sauce
Kosher salt

UNLOCK
THE PAST

For the salsa, purée 2/3 cup of the pineapple. Pour into a bowl. Add remaining pineapple and salsa ingredients and mix well.

For the tartar dressing, blend ginger oil and wasabi paste in a bowl. Add a mixture of next 3 ingredients. Combine lime juice and remaining ingredients; mix well. Mix all together and add to the ginger oil mixture. Blend together and whisk all of above together. May be stored in refrigerator if leftover.

Yield: 8 servings

Ricky Pigg, Joe's 2nd Street Bistro

CIVIL WAR VETERANS

BATHING BEACH

S-312

AT FERNANDINA BEACH, FLORIDA

5A-H751

Sweet Summer Heat Sauce

8	ounces sour cream
4	ounces sweet chili sauce
4	ounces coconut milk
1	teaspoon Sriracha sauce
2	ounces crushed pineapple
1	tablespoon chopped fresh basil
2	teaspoons lime juice
1	teaspoon salt
1	teaspoon paprika

Mix all ingredients together thoroughly in a bowl. Use as a dipping sauce for chicken fingers, fried calamari, shrimp, or other appetizers. This also makes a delicious dressing for slaw.

Yield: 2 1/3 cups

The Oceanside Grill, Omni Amelia Island Plantation

BOOMER: THE CARRIAGE HORSE

Granny's Slaw

1	package shredded cabbage
1	cup seedless grapes
1	cup sliced bananas
1	cup cubed cantaloupe or any fruit that is in season
1	cup grated coconut
1	cup fresh pineapple chunks
1/2	cup mayonnaise

Combine the shredded cabbage, grapes, and bananas in a serving bowl. Add the cantaloupe, coconut, and pineapple chunks. Spoon the mayonnaise over the slaw and toss gently to coat. Chill in the refrigerator until ready to serve.

Yield: 8 servings

Florida House Inn Pimento Cheese with Sesame Crackers

8	ounces shredded Cheddar cheese
1/2	cup mayonnaise
1	tablespoon Dijon mustard
1	tablespoon garlic powder
1/4	teaspoon white pepper
2	tablespoons minced fresh parsley
1/2	cup finely diced pimentos
1/4	cup finely diced white onion

Combine the cheese, mayonnaise, mustard, garlic powder, and white pepper in a large bowl and mix well. Fold in the parsley, pimentos, and onion. Chill in the refrigerator. Serve with sesame crackers.

Yield: 2 cups

Florida House Inn

UNLOCK
THE PAST

IN MEMORY OF
RAYMOND JENCKES REID
DIED MAY 6. 1864.

FRANCIS PRESTON WELLFORD, M.D.
Born in Fredericksburg, Va.
Sept 12. 1829.
JAMES CARMICHAEL HERNDON, M.D.
Born in Fredericksburg, Va.
Sept 22. 1831.
Died in the faithful discharge of their duty at Fernandina,
Florida. Oct. 18. 1877.

STAINED GLASS WINDOWS —
ST. PETER'S EPISCOPAL CHURCH

Peel 'n' Eat Shrimp

3	pounds (21 to 25 count), unpeeled, headless shrimp		1	pound unsalted butter
1	gallon orange juice		2	cups Old Bay Seasoning
3	lemons, cut into halves		1	cup Kosher salt
3	limes, cut into halves		1/2	cup black pepper
2	gallons water		1/4	cup Texas Pete

Make sure shrimp are thawed and rinsed properly. Combine all other ingredients into a large pot and mix thoroughly. Bring to a boil and let simmer for 10 minutes.

Fill a large bowl with ice water. Add shrimp to the pot on the stove and cook for 3 to 5 minutes. It is important that you do not overcook the shrimp.

With a strainer or slotted spoon, remove the shrimp from the pot and place into the ice water. Allow to cool completely. Serve over ice with lemon and cocktail sauce.

Note — You may keep the cooking liquid up to 3 days if refrigerated properly. Just reheat to a boil to use again.

Yield: 3 pounds shrimp

Recipe from The Salty Pelican

Steamboat House — South 10th Street

PRESCOTT HOUSE — NORTH 6TH STREET

GOLF CLUB OF AMELIA — SUMMER BEACH

Palace Saloon

Watermelon-Vodka Italian Ice

1	personal-size seedless watermelon
1/2	cup sugar
1/4	cup vodka

Slice watermelon and chop into small chunks, reserving some good looking slices for garnish. Combine watermelon, sugar and vodka in a bowl. Chill in freezer for two hours. Smash with a whisk. Repeat until it forms a fine icy consistency. Serve in a frozen martini glass garnished with a small slice of watermelon or mint sprig.

Yield: 8 servings

Tim Seyda, BarZin Restaurant

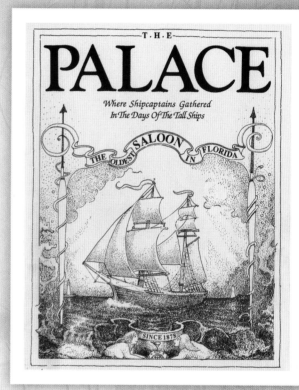

T·H·E

PALACE

Where Shipcaptains Gathered
In The Days Of The Tall Ships

THE OLDEST SALOON IN FLORIDA

SINCE 1878

The Brookie

BROWNIE BATTER

1 3/4 cups semisweet chocolate
1   cup unsalted butter
1   cup sugar
4   eggs
Pinch of salt
1 1/2 teaspoons vanilla extract
1   cup all-purpose flour

COOKIE DOUGH

1   cup unsalted butter
Generous 1/2 cup granulated sugar
Generous 1/2 cup packed brown
      sugar
1   egg
1/2   teaspoon vanilla extract
1/2   teaspoon salt
Generous 1 cup flour
1/2   teaspoon baking soda
1   cup chocolate chips

BROWNIE BATTER

Preheat oven to 300 degrees. Melt chocolate and butter together in a small saucepan. In a separate bowl whip together sugar, eggs, salt, and vanilla to combine. Pour chocolate into eggs. Add flour; mix well. Set mixture aside.

COOKIE DOUGH

Cream together butter and sugars in a bowl of electric mixer until light and fluffy. Slowly add egg one at a time, beating and scraping after each addition. Add vanilla and salt. Add flour and soda and mix until combined. Scrape down bowl and add chocolate chips.

UNLOCK
THE PAST

Assemble Brookie by filling a greased muffin cups ¾ full with brownie batter. Use a small scoop or spoon to create a ball of cookie dough. Place the cookie dough in the center of the brownie batter. Push the cookie dough down halfway into the brownie batter. Bake at 300 degrees for 30 minutes. Let cool completely before removing.

Yield: approximately 12 large or 24 miniature

The Falcon's Nest,
Omni Amelia Island Plantation

Shrimp Fettuccine

16   to 20 shrimp (4 or 5 per person)
1   small shallot, minced
2   garlic cloves, minced
Oil for sautéeing
1/2   cup white wine
1/2   to 3/4 cup each julienned yellow squash,
      zucchini, and carrots
1   teaspoon tomato paste
1/2   cup heavy cream
4   ounces fettuccine pasta
Grated parmesan cheese
Chopped fresh parsley

In a hot sauté pan, cook the shrimp, shallot and garlic in oil, being careful not to burn or brown the garlic. Add the vegetables and tomato paste and cook until tender. Deglaze the pan with white wine. Add the heavy cream and cook until reduced by half. In the meantime, cook the fettuccine according the package directions. Add pasta to shrimp mixture. Season with salt and pepper to taste. Serve topped with grated Parmesan and chopped parsley.

For an even more elegant dish, add the meat from one lobster tail per person when cooking the shrimp.

Yield: 4 servings

Bill Mertens, Gourmet Gourmet

FERNANDINA—WHERE SHRIMP RULE

The picturesque shrimp boats docked at Fernandina Beach's harbor are reminders of the glory days of Amelia Island's thriving shrimping industry. Sadly, what was once a worldwide business has been reduced to local markets as farm-raised and vastly inferior shrimp have flooded the market.

These tiny crustaceans in their wild form have sustained people for thousands of years. Long before Europeans ever reached the north Florida coast, the native Timucuan Indians caught shrimp in cleverly woven weirs. The waters were rich in tiny and white shrimp.

The settlers from foreign lands soon learned how to catch the tasty shrimp and sought to create business opportunities in the export of the delicate morsels.

The challenges were many. The shrimp had to be caught in large quantities, preserved, and shipped to market. The arrival of Solecito Salvatore of Syracuse, Sicily, and his entrepreneurial innovations brought the changes that made Amelia Island a shrimping capital.

The shrimpers loved to have yearly family gatherings and began to race their boats in 1964. Their celebrations and races evolved into the island's annual Isle of Eight Flags Shrimp Festival held each year the first weekend in May.

The shrimping industry has been greatly challenged by the importing of farm raised shrimp. Local restaurants continue to support shrimpers who still venture out into the deeper waters off Amelia Island to harvest the mouth-watering shrimp that can not be matched by any artificially produced shrimp.

Meyer Lemon Relish

Peel and pulp from 1 large Meyer lemon
1   shallot, 1/2 minced, 1/2 very thinly sliced
2   tablespoons fresh lemon juice
1   tablespoon white wine vinegar
1   garlic clove, minced
2   tablespoons minced chives
1   tablespoon finely chopped parsley
1/2 cup extra virgin olive oil
Pinch of crushed red pepper
Salt and freshly ground black pepper

Finely chop the lemon pulp, discarding any seeds. Slice half the peel very thinly; discard remaining peel. Transfer to a bowl and add the remaining ingredients; mix lightly. Relish can be made ahead and refrigerated for up to three days. Serve with fish, pork, or chicken.

Yield: **One cup**

Lisa Waas, food writer for Jacksonville's Florida Times-Union

Shrimp Salad

1	pound shrimp, peeled and deveined
1	teaspoon Old Bay seasoning
1/2	lemon
1/3	cup chopped celery
1/3	cup mayonnaise

Boil shrimp in mixture of Old Bay, lemon, and water until firm. Drain and chill in refrigerator.

While shrimp are chilling, process celery in food processor and remove to bowl. Pulse shrimp in food processor until chunky. Combine the shrimp, celery, mayonnaise, and a pinch of Old Bay and mix well.

Serves 6

Café Karibo

UNLOCK
THE PAST

Florida Snapper en Papillote

Each ingredient listed below is per serving.

1	sheet parchment paper
1	ounce or one handful fresh spinach
5	ounces Red Snapper, seasoned with salt and pepper
1	teaspoon fresh lemon juice
6	Kalamata olives, chopped
1	tablespoon chopped red onion
10	capers, chopped

1	pepperoncini, chopped
2	leaves of fresh basil, chopped
1	tablespoon extra virgin olive oil
2	slices ripe tomato, sliced 1/2 inch thick
	Kosher salt to taste
	Black pepper to taste

Preheat oven to 425 degrees. Fold parchment in half. Cut large (size of fish x 2 plus 2") half heart on fold; unfold. Place the spinach centered on one half. Place fish on top of spinach and add lemon juice. In small bowl, combine the olives, red onion, capers, pepperoncini, basil, olive oil and mix well. Spoon mixture on top of fish and top with tomatoes.

Fold the parchment over to meet the edges over the fish. Start at the top of the heart and fold edges of parchment, sealing edges with narrow folds, twist the tail of heart tightly when you reach the bottom of the heart. Ensure it is airtight so fish will steam properly. Place on flat baking sheet. Bake for 15 minutes. Place the *en papillote* in shallow bowl, open the parchment, and serve.

Yield: 1 portion

Ritz–Carlton, Amelia Island

UNLOCK THE PAST

SCENIC POOL — RITZ-CARLTON, AMELIA ISLAND

Spicy Pirate Gumbo
Amelia Island Museum of History-Style

3/4	cup peanut oil, divided
2	cups celery cut, into ½ inch slices
2	cups onions, cut into ½ inch pieces
2	cups carrots, cut into ½ inch slices
2	cups andouille sausage cut into ½ inch slices
2	cups boneless skinless chicken thighs cut into one inch cubes and dried with a towel
5	quarts chicken stock (reserve three cups)
1/4	cup Tony Chachere's Roux Mix
	Tony Chachere's Creole seasoning
1	pound (31 to 35 count) shrimp, cleaned and deveined
10	cups cooked rice

Heat 1/4 cup of the peanut oil in large frying pan until shimmering. Add vegetables, stir and cover. Cook until celery is soft and carrots and onions are brown, stirring frequently. Transfer to separate bowl.

Return frying pan to medium heat. Add 1/4 cup peanut oil and heat until shimmering. Add sausage. Cook for two minutes or until sausage is deep brown but not burned. Turn; cook other side and transfer cooked pieces to separate bowl. Return frying pan to medium heat. Add 1/4 cup peanut oil and heat until shimmering. Add chicken in batches so it is not crowded. Cook for two minutes or until the cooked side is deep brown without being burned. Turn and cook the other side. Repeat until all chicken is cooked. Transfer to separate bowl.

UNLOCK THE PAST

Place stock (reserving 3 cups) into large pot on medium heat. When stock begins to bubble, add vegetables. Bring back to slight boil. Add prepared sausage and chicken. Lower heat to medium and cook for 40 minutes.

Place dry Tony Chachere's prepackaged roux into one-quart saucepan. Slowly whisk in 3 cups of reserved stock. Cook until a a smooth dark brown slurry forms, stirring constantly. Remove pot from heat. Slowly add 1 cup of slurry to the stock-pot, mixing thoroughly. (If you want to serve thin gumbo, stop the roux addition.)

Repeat, adding slurry until you have the thickness you desire. A thin coat on a wooden spoon will give you a product that will soak into rice without being a soup. If gumbo becomes too thick, add 1/2 cup water or more or until consistency is reached.

Season to taste with Creole seasoning. Add shrimp and cook for 5 minutes. Serve over rice.

Yield: 12 hearty servings

Stuart Davis, Amelia Island Museum of History

THE JAIL HOUSE ROCKS

The Amelia Island Museum of History is located in a most unlikely place—the original Nassau County Jail. Looking at the solid brick building, it is clear it was built to be secure. The jail was built in 1878 at a critical time in the history of Amelia Island. In the years before the Civil War, Fernandina was one of the largest towns in Florida. It had the reputation of being a rough and crude port town. Through the years, it attracted pirates, slave traders, and other unsavory characters. In the beginning of the Golden Age (1870-1910), the little town of Fernandina was entirely transformed. It became a luxurious winter resort for the rich and famous of the great American cities. In keeping with the times, the county built a grand and solid jail.

The Nassau County Jail is an integral and prominent part of the history of Nassau County. The Amelia Island Museum of History opened its doors to visitors in 1986 and trained docents have continued to tell the story of the Eight Flags over Amelia Island and the history of the old jail. The building was added to the National Register of Historic Places in 2009. The Amelia Island Museum of History is open seven days a week and serves over 20,000 people each year.

AMELIA ISLAND
MUSEUM
OF HISTORY
UNLOCK THE PAST

GOLF CLUB OF AMELIA

Fish Tacos

1	cup extra virgin olive oil		4	pieces of 4-ounce snapper or flounder fillets, skin off
1	lemon, zested and juiced		1	cup flour
1	lime, zested and juiced		Sea salt and freshly ground pepper	
2	cloves of garlic		4	large flour tortillas
3	sprigs each thyme and oregano		Corn Relish	
Pinch of cayenne			Cilantro Sauce	
1	onion, sliced thin			

Combine olive oil, lemon zest and juice, lime zest and juice, garlic, herbs, cayenne, and onion in a large zip-lock bag. Add fish and mix ingredients around. Remove air from the bag and close. Marinate 1 hour. Drain. Dredge fish and onions in flour. Shake off excess. Deep-fry at 350 degrees until fish and onions float, about 2 to 3 minutes. Drain on paper towel-lined plate. Season with salt and pepper. Place fish in large flour tortilla. Cover with sauce and relish and roll up.

Note: For a healthier option, grill fish and onions.

CORN RELISH

Corn kernels of 2 ears, roasted			1/2	tablespoon extra virgin olive oil
1/4	cup crumbled feta cheese		1	tablespoon Champagne vinegar
1	red pepper, small dice		Sea salt and freshly ground pepper	
2	tablespoons butter, melted			

Combine all ingredients in a bowl. Refrigerate if made ahead. Serve at room temperature.

CILANTRO SAUCE

1/2   *bunch cilantro, chopped*
4   *cloves garlic, roasted*
1   *cup Greek yogurt*
3   *tablespoons white wine
      vinegar*
1   *pinch sugar*
*Sea salt and freshly ground
      pepper*

Combine all ingredients in a bowl; mix
well.

Yield: 4 servings

Rick Laughlin, Salt Restaurant,
Ritz–Carlton, Amelia Island

FERNANDINA BASE BALL CLUB,
CHAMPIONS OF FLORIDA.
SEPT. 22, 1894.

Never-Fail Ginger Snap Cookies

3/4	cup shortening		1½	teaspoons baking soda
1	cup sugar		1	teaspoon ground cloves
1	egg		1	teaspoon cinnamon
1/4	cup molasses		1	teaspoon ginger
2	cups flour		1/2	cup sugar

Preheat oven 350

Cream shortening and 1 cup sugar together in a mixing bowl. Add whole egg and molasses and beat until smooth. Sift dry ingredients together and add to mixture, beating until smooth. Shape into teaspoon-size balls and roll in 1/2 cup sugar. Place on ungreased cookie sheet. Bake at 350 for 8 to 10 minutes

Yield: 8 to 9 dozen cookies

HISTORIC COURT HOUSE

Goat Cheese Vinaigrette

1   teaspoon chopped garlic
1   cup apple cider vinegar
2   tablespoons Dijon mustard
2   tablespoons honey
1/4   cup lemon juice
1/2   cup white wine
Olive oil
Salt and pepper
Fresh parsley and thyme, finely chopped
3   ounces goat cheese, softened

Combine first 5 ingredients together with wine in a bowl, whisking slowly. Slowly whisk in enough olive oil to make vinaigrette. Add salt, pepper, parsley, and thyme. Add softened goat cheese and blend thoroughly.

Yield: 2 1/2 cups

Brett Carter, Brett's Waterway Cafe and PLAE

POST OFFICE AND CUSTOMS HOUSE · FERNANDINA, FLA.

CLINE
2-C-83

Crab Trap Crab Soup

1	medium onion, chopped
1	green bell pepper, chopped
3	stalks celery, chopped
4	tablespoons butter
1	can evaporated milk
1/2	gallon (8 cups) whole milk
1	pound crab meat, lump or claw

Garlic salt to taste
Salt and Pepper to taste

In a large pot, sauté vegetables in butter for a few minutes. Stir in evaporated milk, whole milk, and crab. Add seasonings. Additional butter may be added for a richer stew. Heat thoroughly but do not let come to a boil. Enjoy with saltines or oyster crackers.

Yield: 8 to 10 servings

The Crab Trap Restaurant

Cheese Wafers

1 cup packed grated extra sharp
   Cheddar, at room temperature
1 stick butter, softened
1 cup flour

1/2 teaspoon salt
1/4 to1/2 teaspoon red pepper
1 cup Rice Krispies

Preheat oven to 350 degrees. Mix softened cheese and butter in a bowl. Sift together flour, salt, and red pepper and combine with butter mixture; mix well. Stir in Rice Krispies. Roll into balls; place on ungreased cookie sheet. Then flatten with a fork. Bake until lightly brown.

Cook for 10-15 minutes until light brown.

Yield: 24 to 36 wafers

FIRST ARTILLERY COMPANY OF NASSAU LIGHT ARTILLERY

Morning Glory Muffins

2	cups all-purpose flour
1 1/4	cups sugar
2	teaspoons baking soda
2	teaspoons cinnamon
1/2	teaspoon salt
1 1/2	cups finely grated carrots
1 1/2	cups finely grated peeled Granny Smith apples
3/4	cup finely chopped coconut
1/2	cup finely chopped dates
1/2	cup finely chopped pecans
3	eggs, beaten
1	cup vegetable oil
1/2	teaspoon vanilla extract

Preheat oven to 375 degrees. Mix the flour, sugar, baking soda, cinnamon, and salt in a large bowl. Combine the carrots, apples, coconut, dates and pecans in a bowl and mix well. Stir in the eggs, oil and vanilla. Add to the flour mixture and stir until moistened. Spoon into buttered and floured miniature muffin pans. Bake for 11 to 15 minutes or until a tester inserted near the center comes out clean.

Yield: 40 to 48 miniature muffins

Micah's Place Auxiliary, *A Savory Place* cookbook (Micah's Place is the Nassau County Shelter for victims of domestic violence)

Granny Mutt's Blueberry Squares

1	stick unsalted butter
1	cup packed brown sugar
1	cup granulated sugar
2	eggs
2	teaspoons vanilla extract
2	cups all-purpose flour
2	teaspoons baking powder
1/2	teaspoon salt
1	cup fresh blueberries
1	cup chopped pecans
Cinnamon sugar	

Melt butter in a saucepan. Stir in remaining ingredients in order listed. Spread into a well-greased 9x13-inch baking pan. Generously sprinkle cinnamon sugar on top. Bake at 350 degrees for 30 to 35 minutes. Cut into squares.

Serve warm topped with vanilla ice cream.

Yield: 1 dozen

Kelley's Courtyard Cafe

BATHING BEAUTIES

CENTRE STREET 1868

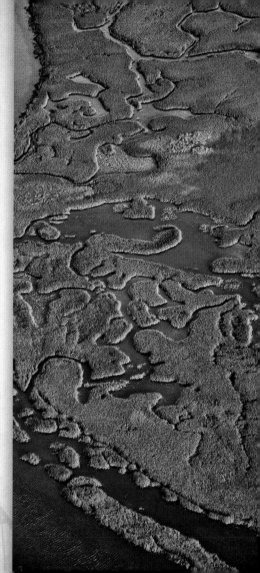

Pink Pears

1	bottle of red wine
2	cinnamon sticks
3	star anise
1	vanilla bean, split
4	cloves
1	cup sugar
1	sliced orange
Rind of one lemon	
6	ripe Comice pears

For the syrup, bring all the ingredients except the pears to a boil in large stockpot, stirring gently until the sugar is dissolved. Lower the heat, allowing the mixture to infuse.

Peel the pears and add to the syrup. Let them to cook over low heat for at least 30 minutes. The longer they stay in to syrup, the darker they will become. Remove the pears with a slotted spoon.

Strain the syrup and cook to reduce to half its volume. Serve over the pears.

Yield: 6 servings

Brett Carter, Brett's Waterway Cafe and PLAE

Happy Tomato Chicken Salad

1/2	cup mayonnaise
1	tablespoon grainy mustard
1/4	teaspoon white pepper
1/4	teaspoon celery salt
2	cups chopped cooked chicken
1/2	cup chopped pecans
1/2	cup pineapple tidbits
1	hard-boiled egg, chopped
1	celery stalk, chopped

Combine mayonnaise, mustard, white pepper and celery salt in a bowl; mix to blend. Add chicken, pecans, pineapple, egg and celery; mix gently. Chill in refrigerator. Serve on lettuce leaves.

Yield: 2 to 3 servings

Happy Tomato Courtyard Cafe and BBQ

N.B.

VILLA LAS PALMAS, HOME OF M. D. BORDEN.   FERNANDINA, FLA.

Prosciutto-Wrapped Scallops with Chimichurri Mayonnaise

2	cups cornmeal
20	fresh medium size scallops
10	slices prosciutto, thinly sliced
20	toothpicks/skewers
	Vegetable oil for frying

Place cornmeal into a mixing bowl. Add scallops and toss to coat completely. Cut prosciutto into halves lengthwise. Wrap prosciutto around each scallop and insert toothpick to secure. Deep-fry at 375 degrees for 3 to 4 minutes or until prosciutto is crispy. (Scallops can be prepared several days ahead of time before frying.). Serve with Chimichurri Mayonnaise (page 104).

Yield: 4 to 5 servings

The Ritz–Carlton, Amelia Island

**GRAVESIDE ANGEL—
BOSQUE BELLO CEMETERY**

Chimichurri Mayonnaise

1	cup chopped parsley
1/4	cup chopped fresh cilantro
4	cloves of garlic, peeled
3	tablespoons red wine vinegar
3	bay leaves
1/2	cup olive oil
1/4	teaspoon red pepper flakes
1/4	teaspoon kosher salt
1	cup mayonnaise

Place all ingredients except mayonnaise into a blender container and process until smooth. Place mayonnaise in mixing bowl and gradually add chimichurri to desired taste. Chimichurri mayonnaise will last up to two weeks when refrigerated.

Yield: 4 to 5 servings

The Ritz–Carlton, Amelia Island

UNLOCK THE PAST

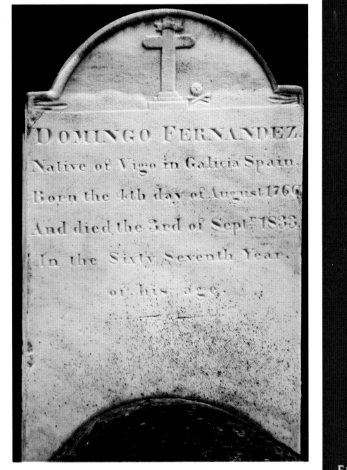

FERNANDEZ TOMBSTONE

A fish story

Total number 42
Drum 36
Bass 6
Total weight 1890
April 19 - 07

Fernandina Florida

Blackened Grouper with Black Beans and Coconut Rice

2	tablespoons olive oil plus more for sautéeing
1	cup Jasmine rice
1/2	teaspoon salt
1	can coconut milk plus 1/2 can water
1/4	cup chopped red pepper
1/4	cup chopped onion
2	tablespoons chopped ginger
2	tablespoons chopped garlic
1/2	cup chicken broth
1	14.5 ounce can black beans, drained
1/2	cup corn kernels
1	tablespoon curry paste
4	to 8 pieces of grouper, cleaned and trimmed
4	tablespoons Seafood Magic
8	large, peeled and deveined shrimp

Preheat oven to 400 degrees. In a saucepan combine 2 tablespoons of olive oil and rice. Cook over a high-medium flame and mix until rice is evenly coated. Add salt, coconut milk, and water and bring to a boil. Let boil for 1 minute; reduce heat to a low simmer. Cover and cook for 25 minutes. Remove from heat and remove cover. Coat a skillet with 2 tablespoons olive oil. Sauté pepper, onion, ginger and garlic over medium-high heat until onion is translucent. Add chicken broth, drained beans, corn, and curry paste.

Coat one side of grouper with a tablespoon of Seafood Magic and place seasoned side down on a very hot skillet. Leave fish alone until nicely blackened and comes off pan easily. Flip over the fish and place in oven to finish for 4 to 5 minutes. Grill shrimp. Keep an eye on them. Arrange grouper on rice and vegetables. Garnish with 2 shrimp.

Yield: 4 servings

Tim Seyda, BarZin Restaurant

UNLOCK THE PAST

Coconut-Chicken Balls

8	ounces cream cheese, softened	2	tablespoons mayonnaise
1	cup finely chopped cooked chicken	1	tablespoon curry powder
		2	to 3 tablespoons chopped chutney
1	cup slivered almonds, finely ground	1/2	teaspoon Lawrey's seasoned salt
			Grated coconut

Combine cream cheese, chicken, almonds, mayonnaise, curry powder, chutney, and seasoned salt in a bowl and mix well. Chill, covered, in the refrigerator. Shape into small balls and roll in the coconut. Chill until serving time. Arrange on a serving plate with wooden picks for serving.

Yield: about three dozen

Micah's Place Auxiliary, *A Savory Place Cookbook* (Micah's Place is the Nassau County shelter for victims of domestic violence)

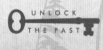

PIPPI LONGSTOCKING HOUSE — OLD TOWN

HIRTH FAMILY OUTING

Verandah Sweet Corn Soup

2 1/2	pounds fresh raw corn kernels, cobs reserved	6	ounces diced carrot
2 1/2	tablespoons salt	1/2	cup chopped garlic
1/4	pound whole butter	1	teaspoon white pepper
1	pound onions, diced	1/2	gallon corn broth
1/2	pound celery, diced	1	quart cream
1/4	pound leeks, julienned	1	ounce basil, tied into a sachet

Place reserved corn cobs and 1/2 gallon water in large pot. Bring to boil. Reduce heat and simmer for 15 minutes. Season broth with salt. Strain broth, discarding the solids.

Combine next seven ingredients in stock-pot. Sweat over medium heat until moisture evaporates. Add broth, cream, and basil sachet and simmer for 30 minutes. Remove the sachet. Purée in a blender or processor, then strain through a fine mesh strainer. Serve warm.

Yield: 12 servings

The Verandah Restaurant, Omni Amelia Island Plantation

UNLOCK
THE PAST

Omni-Amelia Island Plantation Tennis Center

Lemon-Honey Tart
with Salted Shortbread Crust

CRUST

Nonstick vegetable oil spray

1³/4 cups all-purpose flour

2   tablespoons cornstarch

1¹/4 teaspoons kosher salt

1¹/2 sticks unsalted butter, cut into
       1 inch pieces, softened

2/3   cup confectioner's sugar

FILLING

1   Meyer lemon or thin-skinned
       regular lemon

1   cup sugar

*Leaves from 2 thyme sprigs,
 chopped*

3   tablespoons honey

1   tablespoon finely grated
       lemon zest

3   large eggs

2   large egg yolks

1/4   cup all-purpose flour

2   teaspoons cornstarch

1/4   teaspoon kosher salt

2/3   cup fresh lemon juice,
       preferably Meyer lemon

For the crust, coat a 9-inch springform pan with nonstick spray. Whisk flour, cornstarch, and salt in a small bowl and set aside. Pulse butter and confectioner sugar in a food processor until smooth. Add dry ingredients and pulse until mixture resembles medium-size pebbles. (Dough will not come together completely). Transfer dough to prepared pan. Using fingers, press dough evenly onto bottom of pan and 1 ½ inches up sides. Crust can be prepared one day ahead. Cover and chill.

Place crust pan on rack in upper third of oven, pre-heated to 325 degrees. Bake for 30 to 40 minutes or until center is firm to the touch and edges are beginning to turn golden brown.

UNLOCK
THE PAST

For the filling, using a mandoline, slice lemon into paper-thin rounds. Remove seeds. Mix sugar, thyme, honey and zest in a bowl. Add lemon slices, toss to coat. Set aside for 30 to 40 minutes until lemon is softened and sugar is dissolved. When crust is almost done, whisk eggs and yolks to blend. Whisk mixture of flour, cornstarch, and salt into egg mixture. Whisk in lemon juice. Add lemon slice mixture and mix gently. Reduce oven temperature to 300 degrees. Pour filling into hot crust.

Bake for 25 to 30 minutes until filling is set and slightly puffed around the edges. Cool on a wire rack. Chill for four hours or longer. Remove the side of the pan to unmold onto serving plate.

Yield: 8 to 10 servings

Lisa Waas, food writer for Jacksonville's Florida Times-Union

115

Pat's Olives

1	jar queen-sized pimento-stuffed olives
1	8-ounce block cream cheese
	Finely chopped pecans

Soften the cream cheese a bit. Drain the olives and pat dry. Cover each olive with cream cheese. Roll in pecans. Chill until serving time. Cut olives into halves. Serve with the cut side up so the olive shows in the middle.

Yield: 40

TROLLEY — FERNANDINA BEACH

Grilled Romaine Salad with Fried Oysters

2	hearts of romaine
4	tablespoons olive oil
8	large oysters, shucked
1	can beer
Seafood breading mix	
1	cup cooking oil for frying
1	red onion
1	small wheel Brie cheese
Caesar salad dressing (can use store-bought)	
2	tablespoons curry powder

Preheat the grill. Clean and trim romaine hearts and cut tips off of leaf ends. Split heads lengthwise into halves. Drizzle cut sides with olive oil and grill until nicely marked. Dunk oysters in beer, then in the seafood breading. Fry oysters in cooking oil in a skillet until lightly browned. Thinly slice the red onion and separate into rings. Cut brie into small chunks. Arrange romaine, oysters, onion and brie on large salad plate. Blend Caesar dressing with curry powder until completely mixed. Serve with the salad.

Yield: 4 servings

Tim Seyda, BarZin Restaurant

Shrimp Scampi with Sun-dried Tomato Compound Butter

2	tablespoons white wine
1	stick salted butter, softened
2	tablespoons Dijon mustard (1/8 cup)
1/3	cup finely chopped sun-dried tomatoes (drained of oil and patted dry)
1	tablespoon brandy
1 1/2	teaspoons lemon juice

Chopped parsley (1 to 2 tablespoons to taste)
Chopped basil (1 to 2 tablespoons to taste)
1/2 teaspoon red pepper flakes
2 pounds peeled and deveined shrimp
Handful of fresh spinach per person

Combine first 6 ingredients in mixer bowl or food processor. Beat or process until smooth. Add herbs and red pepper flakes. Mix thoroughly. Sauté shrimp with 3 to 4 tablespoons of the compound butter for approximately 2 1/2 minutes until shrimp are opaque and firm to the touch. Do not overcook.

Serve in bowls over fresh spinach. Spinach will wilt slightly. Serve with crusty bread and extra compound butter for dipping.

Note: If the butter compound gets too hot and separates in the sauté pan, add a splash of wine to pull it back together.

Yield: 4 servings as an entree salad; 6 to 8 as a pre-dinner salad.

Brett Carter, Brett's Waterway Cafe and PLAE

Centre Street at night

CREDITS

DICKIE ANDERSON

Dickie Anderson brings her many talents and passion for Amelia Island's history to her writing. She is a trained docent and volunteer at the Amelia Island Museum of History, has served on the boards of the Amelia Arts Academy, the Amelia Island Chamber Music Festival and served as Executive Director of the Amelia Island Book Festival. Her column, *From The Porch*, appears weekly in the *Fernandina Beach Newsleader*. Her articles on the people and history of Amelia Island are featured in regional publications including the *Amelia Islander Magazine*. Anderson has published four collections of her popular column. Anderson's most recent book, *Great Homes of Fernandina, Architectural Treasures of Amelia Island's Golden Age*, was published in November of 2012.

LISA WAAS

Lisa lives with her husband Joseph and two children in a family home built in 1886 in the historic district of Fernandina Beach. The couple did extensive remodeling of the historic house. They share a passion for cooking and when it came time for the remodel, along with a doubling of the main kitchen, a special baking kitchen was added. Lisa began writing for the Jacksonville's *Florida Times-Union* as a feature writer in 2010. Her stories share insights into her experiences in the kitchen, on life and family and recipes.

STEPHAN LEIMBERG

Stephan R. Leimberg, Amelia Island photographer, is known for his breath-taking photographs of birds, flowers and landscapes. His work can be found in Amelia Island galleries. Leimberg was named the 2008 International Nikon – Popular Photography Mentor Series Grand Prize Winner. Leimberg produced the popular FACES OF AMELIA, a series of photos of Amelia Island notables. His portraits have been featured as book covers or author pictures and include a portrait of Pat Conroy used in his book *My Life In Reading*. Steve and his wife JoAnn are active in Wild Amelia, the Amelia Island Museum of History and Friends of the Library. His work can be viewed on his website—www.Unseemimages.com.

AMELIA ISLAND MUSEUM OF HISTORY

Teen Peterson, museum curator and Judy Pillans, museum volunteer coordinated the museum's invaluable contributions to *Meet Me on™ Amelia Island*. Thanks to Phyllis Davis, Executive Director and the staff at the Amelia Island Museum of History.

Thanks to Jan Johannes, photographer, and Sweetpea Productions for the use of pictures from *Great Houses of Fernandina, Architectural Treasures from Amelia Island's Golden Age*.

RECIPE INDEX

UNLOCK
THE PAST

Amelia Island
Museum of History

The Amelia Island Museum of History (AIMH) is dedicated to the education about and preservation of artifacts which represent all forms of life and culture in Nassau County. Its mission is "to bring alive and preserve the area's rich history" and it sees itself as the caretaker and disseminator of that exciting local history.

In 1975, historically-minded local residents realized that Nassau County lacked an organization to preserve and care for local historical artifacts. Being the site of some of the nation's earliest European activity, there was no agency in place to care for the myriad of historical items or maintain the wealth of historical information that was available in the community. With this need in mind, the group founded the "Fernandina Historical Museum" in the old train depot. After a new jail facility was built in 1979, Nassau County officials offered the historic Nassau County Jail Building to the Museum. To do this, the AIMH worked with a number of community leaders and developed strong ties to local schools, businesses, and other non-profits to access community needs and maximize impact.

The museum's 2013 current staff consists of four professional full-time staff, a part-time collections manager, three part-time auxiliary staff, and boasts

214 active volunteers. The museum's collection contains over 4,200 items and includes: photographs, books, documents, maps, objects, and digitally recorded oral histories. The museum is currently working to digitize its collection, and currently has approximately 75% of it available to the public online. The museum is also involved in the Veterans History Project which records the rememberances of local veterans as part of the greater effort by the Library of Congress.

Besides professional exhibits, the Museum offers 7 different historical tours of the area, and several educational evening programs each month which are well attended. In addition the museum offers a children's summer program as well as other programs throughout the year. The museum also regularly partners with other area civic organizations such as the Fernandina Beach Public Library, the Amelia Island Film Festival, and the Book Island Festival to bring educational activities to the community. The museum's annual attendance has steadily been rising over the years with approximately 20,000 visitors in 2010.

For more information go to
www.ameliamuseum.org

AMELIA ISLAND
MUSEUM
OF HISTORY
UNLOCK THE PAST

The Amelia Island Museum of History
is located at 233 South Third Street,
Fernandina Beach, Florida.
Phone: (904) 261-7378

UNLOCK
THE PAST